Not by Bread Alone

Daily Reflections for Lent 2022

Amy Ekeh and Thomas D. Stegman, SJ

LITURGICAL PRESS

Collegeville, Minnesota

www.litpress.org

Nihil Obstat: Reverend Robert Harren, J.C.L., *Censor deputatus*

Imprimatur: ✝ Most Reverend Donald J. Kettler, J.C.L., D.D., Bishop of Saint Cloud, July 1, 2021

Cover design by Monica Bokinskie. Cover art courtesy of Getty Images.

ISSN: 1552-8782 (print); 2692-6407 (e-book)

ISBN: 978-0-8146-6607-4   978-0-8146-6633-3 (e-book)

Introduction

Lent is about one simple thing: turning to Jesus Christ, and him crucified (1 Cor 2:2). Lent is our time to journey with Christ, to set our own faces to Jerusalem and accompany him to the cross (Luke 9:51). Lent is our time to be with the crucified Lord, and to wait quietly with him for the brilliance of resurrection.

And yet, Lent is more than a solitary walk with Jesus. We do not walk this road to the cross alone. We walk as Church. We walk as people of God, as the Body of Christ (1 Cor 12:27). Yes, everything we do as we travel this road is with and for one another. This is what it means to follow Christ, to witness his death, to be conformed to him and his way of love that the cross embodies. It means to recognize that we belong to each other, that we must also lay down our lives for one another. We learn this at the foot of the cross, and we take it with us into the bright light of Easter.

As a pilgrim Church, we look to the daily Liturgy of the Word as a rich resource to nourish us on our Lenten journey. The book in your hands contains reflections, meditations, and prayers inspired by these daily Scripture readings. As you read and pray with this book each day, you will hear two distinct voices—one a Jesuit priest, the other a married mother of four—voices of two friends and colleagues whose different walks of life intersect in a mutual love of God's word and a shared desire to explore that word with others.

Each day, you will find that one of us has written a reflection, and the other has responded with a meditation and prayer. It is our hope that this ongoing conversation, this daily mixing of voices and perspectives, has enriched our presentation and will draw you into the journey with us. We have been blessed by writing together for you, learning from one another and praying for one another along the way.

Lent is upon us. What will we do with this time, this holy season? Will it be like other Lents, or will it be different? How will we focus our minds and hearts to make the most of this sacred time?

Lent is here. Let's embark on this journey together.

Amy Ekeh
Thomas D. Stegman, SJ

Reflections

Practicing the Faith

Readings: Joel 2:12-18; 2 Cor 5:20–6:2; Matt 6:1-6, 16-18

Scripture:
Behold, now is a very acceptable time; behold, now is the day of salvation. (2 Cor 6:2)

Reflection: My first memory, as a school kid, of receiving ashes from our parish priest is still vivid. His thumb pressed a generous amount on my forehead; several particles fell like dust before my eyes. What I recall most are the words he prayed, so haunting to my young ears: "Remember that you are dust, and to dust you shall return." Those words certainly got my attention. Return to dust?!?

So, too, do some lines from our readings grab our attention. Joel's exhortations ring out with a sense of urgency: "Blow the trumpet in Zion! Proclaim a fast, call an assembly." Paul urges the Corinthians to recognize the importance of the moment: "*now* is the day of salvation"!

It's appropriate that Ash Wednesday grabs our attention so dramatically. Today we embark on our annual Lenten journey in preparation for celebrating the sacred events of our salvation—Jesus' self-offering in love, his resurrection, and the outpouring of the Spirit.

Today's Gospel reading sets forth the traditional Lenten practices: prayer, fasting, and almsgiving. These practices are tried and true, though we should keep their true purposes in mind. *Prayer*: let's set aside more time in quiet to listen to God's word, to heed the Spirit's presence and promptings. *Fasting*: let's reflect honestly on the various ways we attempt to satisfy ourselves, and open spaces within so that God can fill us with what truly satisfies. *Almsgiving*: let's give thanks for the many ways God has been generous to us and imitate that generosity toward those in need.

Now is the time to practice our faith afresh. We will have much to celebrate at journey's end.

—*TS*

Meditation: Today is a day of both penitence and joy. We pause to recognize our sinfulness and our need to repent. At the same time, we are so proud to be marked with the cross. This mark is not shameful; it is our identity. We belong to Christ, and he to us. How will we proclaim that identity this Lent, when the ashes have fallen away?

Prayer: Lord Jesus Christ, be with us every step of the way as we take up this Lenten journey.

—*AE*

It's Our Choice

Readings: Deut 30:15-20; Luke 9:22-25

Scripture:
Moses said to the people: "Today I have set before you life and prosperity, death and doom." (Deut 30:15)

Reflection: My friend Paula's young son is prematurely wise. He has a way of looking her in the eye, laying a calm hand on her shoulder, and matter-of-factly delivering fantastic words to live by. One of Nick's proverbs that we repeat around our house is: *"You always have a choice."* It reminds me of something an old Cistercian professor once told me: "The whole universe could blow up in your face—you could still be saying no."

The power of human free will is astounding. We *always* have a choice. Today's reading from the ancient book of Deuteronomy reminds us of this. Moses tells Israel—faithful, faltering Israel—that a clear choice lies before them: life or death, blessing or curse. For Moses the choice is simple and straightforward: to choose life is to love God, to listen to God, to "hold fast" to God (Deut 30:20). This is the way of blessing.

Of course, we know that in our day-to-day lives these choices are not always so clear. How do we love? How do we listen? How do we hold fast? How do we, as Moses instructs, choose life?

The answers to these questions may not be clear in every circumstance of our lives, but there's beauty and merit in asking them. And there is tremendous value in remembering our own power—our power to choose. God was never interested in automatons or a people coerced into loving him. God only wants our love if it is freely given.

We always have a choice.

—AE

Meditation: The freedom to choose can, at times, lead to paralysis—especially when there are so many options. It can also be a burden, as some choices have significant consequences attached to them. But just imagine if we weren't free to choose. That freedom is a gift from God who, in his love for us, invites us to respond, in big choices and small, with love.

Prayer: Thank you, Lord, for the gift of our dignity to choose. Help me, as I begin this Lenten journey, to be aware of all the choices I make. Inspire me to choose the way of life—for my own sake and for the sake of all whom I encounter.

—TS

March 4: Friday after Ash Wednesday

Proper Fasting

Readings: Isa 58:1-9a; Matt 9:14-15

Scripture:
This, rather, is the fasting that I wish . . .
Sharing your bread with the hungry. (Isa 58:6-7)

Reflection: When I was younger, the first task concerning Lent was to determine, "What am I giving up this year for Lent?" Whether chocolate, soda pop, or (gulp!) desserts, it seemed like a great sacrifice. For many today, such "sacrifice" may seem to miss the point: we should focus on doing something *for* others rather than giving something up.

Nevertheless, giving something up is a form of fasting, one of the Lenten practices (recall the Gospel reading for Ash Wednesday). But what sort of fasting is appropriate? I'm not proud to admit that some years, for Lent, I have refrained from certain foods and drinks, motivated largely by my wish to shed a few pounds. But that made fasting about myself. And that's not what God desires.

The prophet Isaiah proposes appropriate ways of—and reasons for—fasting. Foregoing a fulsome meal and using the money saved to feed others is a salutary fast. Refraining from uttering hurtful words is another. So, too, is fasting from eating or wearing products that are the result of unjust and oppressive labor conditions.

As I suggested on Wednesday, we might also consider fasting from some of the ways we try to satisfy ourselves, or from those things that distract us from focusing on the essentials of life. I recall a retreat master suggesting that I fast from so much time with the sports page. That hit close to home! But it was good advice.

So let's not be too fast to jettison fasting as old-fashioned. There are ways of fasting that are acceptable to the Lord.

—*TS*

Meditation: Reflect on the possible benefits of an "old-fashioned" fast. Does fasting from some particular food, drink, or entertainment distract you from the true purpose of Lent, or does it help to empty you so you may be filled with something greater? Is there room—or benefit—in your Lenten practice for a concrete sacrifice? Different circumstances will call for different responses. Consider yours in prayer.

Prayer: Lord God, you have declared that a true fast consists in nurturing a loving heart and caring for those in need. May all my fasts be true fasts.

—*AE*

A Seat at the Table

Readings: Isa 58:9b-14; Luke 5:27-32

Scripture:
The Pharisees and their scribes complained to his disciples, saying, "Why do you eat and drink with tax collectors and sinners?" (Luke 5:30)

Reflection: It's so easy to dislike the Pharisees! In today's Gospel they come across as they usually do—superior, adversarial, and rude. And worst of all, they don't seem to understand Jesus or his ministry. They don't seem to understand compassion.

Of course, in the Gospel stories, the Pharisees serve as a bit of a foil. Although some of the religious leaders of Jesus' day certainly were corrupt and wished Jesus harm, many of them were simply devout Jews of good conscience who were zealous for the law.

But Jesus was saying and doing something new. It surprised the Pharisees and made them uncomfortable. It did not conform to their interpretations of the law which insisted that sinners—those living outside the law—were to be avoided.

Our first inclination when we read of these encounters between Jesus and the Pharisees is to shake our heads at the Pharisees and join Jesus at the table. Tax collectors and sinners? No problem! We're on Jesus' side!

But imagine for a moment whose table you most want to avoid. Whom do you oppose? Whom do you dislike? Who makes your blood boil? That is whose table Jesus is sitting at today. That is who he is eating and drinking with, having a good time with, entering into relationship with, confirming with his love.

It's easy to imagine ourselves at an old table with Jesus, with a vague sense of the strangers known in that day as sinners. But we live this gospel reality now. The call today is to sit with him at our own tables—political, professional, personal—and to eat and drink in harmony with *all* of our brothers and sisters.

—*AE*

Meditation: Jesus' call to repentance is to all of us, for each one of us has sinned. But, as St. Ignatius of Loyola came to realize profoundly, we are sinners *yet loved by God*. When we allow God's love and forgiveness to sink in, we become more compassionate in the way we view others, and our circle of "companions" (whose meaning derives from "sharing bread") widens.

Prayer: Lord, though I have sinned against you, help me to know your merciful love and forgiveness, so that I may look at others with mercy.

—*TS*

God's Faithful Son

Readings: Deut 26:4-10; Rom 10:8-13; Luke 4:1-13

Scripture:
"If you are the Son of God . . ." (Luke 4:3, 9)

Reflection: The Gospel reading for the First Sunday of Lent is the account of the tempting of Jesus by Satan. This year we hear Luke's version. Jesus is in the wilderness, having fasted for forty days. In the moment of his vulnerability, Satan enters the scene and tempts him to betray his identity and mission.

Notice how Satan begins his first and third tests: "*If you are the Son of God . . .*" Now Luke has made abundantly clear, starting at the scene of the annunciation, that Jesus *is* the Son of God (1:35). At issue, therefore, is not who Jesus is. Rather, the issue is *what kind of Son* will Jesus be?

As the story proceeds, we learn that Jesus is God's beloved Son who is completely faithful to enacting his Father's will. Jesus does not succumb to grasping after life on his own terms ("command this stone to become bread"); he recognizes and trusts that true life comes from God. Jesus does not seek power and prestige ("I shall give to you all this power and glory"); he came to serve, not to be served. And Jesus does not go about glorifying himself; he proclaims the kingdom of God and glorifies his heavenly Father.

We are God's sons and daughters by adoption. Lent affords us the opportunity to grow in fidelity to becoming the child of God each of us is called to be within our own particular vocations. To do so, I need to withstand the many voices and inclinations that lure me from being the person God calls me to be. And, like the psalmist, to rely on God who is "with me . . . when I am in trouble" (91:15).

—TS

Meditation: Our busy, demanding world exposes us to a cacophony of loud, conflicting voices. Many of these voices wear away at us and our fidelity to the God we love. They threaten the core identity we so proudly proclaimed with a smudge of ash at the beginning of our Lenten journey. This Lent, which of these voices can you silence? Which can you reject?

Prayer: Lord Jesus, faithful Son, protect me from voices that lead me away from being the person God has called me to be.

—AE

Holy Like God

Readings: Lev 19:1-2, 11-18; Matt 25:31-46

Scripture:
The LORD said to Moses, "Speak to the whole assembly of the children of Israel and tell them: Be holy, for I, the LORD, your God, am holy." (Lev 19:1-2)

Reflection: What does it mean to be holy like God? God's words to Israel may remind us of Jesus' teaching to "be perfect, just as your heavenly Father is perfect" (Matt 5:48).

These divine standards might strike us as a bit idealistic. But this standard is given to us in a particular context: a loving relationship with the Sacred. God is not waiting to see if we will measure up. Rather, God is inviting us to enter relationships.

Yes, God is holy because God is other—removed, different, transcendent, above all things. But God is also holy because God is with us—present, involved, in-the-mix, totally intertwined with human beings and the messes we make and the beauty we emanate. Holiness is otherness and sameness. It is being different and being with.

In today's Gospel reading, Jesus tells us that we will someday be judged. But we won't be judged on a standard of perfection that looks like a ruler or a scale. Rather, we will be judged on how present we were to others, how in-the-mix we were willing to be, how totally intertwined we were with those who needed us most.

In the words of St. John of the Cross, "At the evening of life, we shall be judged on our love." *Holiness* and *perfection* can be replaced with that one word: *love*. Love is a sacred paradox: it sets us apart from the ways of the world even as it binds us closer to all that God has made.

—AE

Meditation: Moses' exhortation to the Israelites touches upon the issue of vocation. Israel was called to show forth God's holiness—to manifest God's loving ways—to the nations. Similarly, the Church is called to be the sacrament of Christ's love in and for the world. We live out that vocation, as individuals and corporately, when we extend loving help to the hungry, thirsty, stranger, ill-clad, sick, and imprisoned.

Prayer: Lord Jesus, Emmanuel (*God-with-us*), open my eyes and heart to recognize your presence in those who are marginalized, to realize that they are your brothers and sisters. Help me to incarnate your love for them.

—TS

God's Performative Word

Readings: Isa 55:10-11; Matt 6:7-15

Scripture:
[My word] shall do my will,
achieving the end for which I sent it. (Isa 55:11)

Reflection: Today's first reading proclaims the power and efficacy of God's word. God's word does not return to God without achieving his purpose. Theologians refer to this quality of the divine word as "performative." A good example is the first creation story in Genesis 1, where God speaks, and what is spoken comes into being.

Jesus is the Word-made-flesh, the very self-expression of God, who speaks and acts as only God can do (because he is God). What Jesus speaks in today's Gospel, the prayer we call the Lord's Prayer, is a most precious gift. If we allow the words of this prayer to take root in our hearts, we will be transformed, and God's performative word will work through us.

The prayer's opening, "Our Father," teaches that we can regard God as a loving parent who always desires what is for our good. The "Our" reminds us that we belong to a family of faith. To pray for the coming of God's kingdom and the enactment of God's will calls for a commitment on our part to do God's will. How can I pray that God's will be done if I'm not willing to obey God's ways? By becoming obedient children, we give God glory and bear witness to God's holiness.

Our petitions for daily bread and forgiveness manifest two basic truths: we are completely dependent upon God for life; and we are in need of God's mercy. With the gifts of sustenance and forgiveness come the responsibilities of being generous with others and forgiving those who have hurt us.

Let's remember this performative aspect of God's word every time we pray, "Our Father . . ."

—*TS*

Meditation: It may be hard to imagine that a prayer we say so often—the Lord's Prayer—can transform us. And yet these are the words that Jesus himself taught us to pray! Let's say the Our Father today slowly and thoughtfully, imagining ourselves at the feet of Jesus, praying along with his voice. Let's allow ourselves to be transformed by this prayer of Jesus as we journey on toward the cross.

Prayer: Lord Jesus, you speak the words of the Father. Speak and bring about change in us. Transform us with your word.

—*AE*

Sackcloth and Ashes

Readings: Jonah 3:1-10; Luke 11:29-32

Scripture:
When the news reached the king of Nineveh, he rose from his throne, laid aside his robe, covered himself with sackcloth, and sat in the ashes. (Jonah 3:6)

Reflection: Biblical imagery is so rich that just one verse can give us plenty to pray with. Today's reading from Jonah offers us such an image: the king of a great city lays aside the trappings of his office—signs of wealth and power—covers himself with hairy sackcloth, and sits in a pile of ashes. He repents for his own sins and for those of the people.

In the ancient Near East, sackcloth, usually sewn from goats' hair, was used for storing grain or making tents and rugs. As you can imagine, the cloth was quite rough—not something you would typically want to feel against your skin. This dark, rough material was sometimes sewn into garments that were worn in times of deep mourning, heart-wrenching distress, or from-the-gut repentance. To wear such a garment was to declare: *all is not right in my world.*

Repentance is a vulnerable moment. It requires profound humility and a deep wellspring of personal hope. We must be willing to change, and we must believe that forgiveness and new life await us.

The king of Nineveh descended from his throne, set aside his robe, and replaced it with sackcloth. Before all the people—"great and small"—he humbled himself. He wore something dark and uncomfortable. He acknowledged a deep pain. He hoped for change.

In response to the repentance of the king and his people, God "repented" of the destruction he had planned for the city. *God repented?* This is no philosophical quandary about whether the divine mind can change. Rather, it is a promise that God responds to our humility and is worthy of our hope.

—*AE*

Meditation: The word translated as "repented" at the end of today's Gospel reading literally means "to change one's mind" or to turn away from one thing towards another. Jesus is present to us in many ways. How alert am I to turning *towards* him—and away from those things that keep me from him? How does his way of holiness challenge me to change my thinking about people and things?

Prayer: Lord Jesus, help me to be attuned to your presence, to keep my eyes fixed on you and my ears attentive to your teaching. Bless me with the humility to repent.

—*TS*

Power of Prayer

Readings: Esth C:12, 14-16, 23-25; Matt 7:7-12

Scripture:
". . . knock and the door will be opened to you." (Matt 7:7)

Reflection: In a CCD class on prayer, I asked Sr. Elizabeth, "Can I pray for the Green Bay Packers to win?" She assured me I could pray to God for anything. Given how the Pack played back then, I could have concluded that God answered half of my prayers.

Jesus exhorts, "Ask and it will be given to you." Sounds easy, no? Yet we know it's not. At the center of Jesus' teaching is God's desire to give us what we need. Prayer expresses our need for God and our trust in God to provide. Like Esther in today's first reading—at wit's end and left to our own devices—prayer allows us to acknowledge our needs, many of which only God can fulfill.

Prayer is also a way to enact the priestly identity given to us at baptism. Petitionary prayer for others and their needs—especially our loved ones—is a meaningful practice. While we believe God can work miracles, we know that God often works in and through folks like you and me. When I pray for a loved one in need, for instance, I allow God to inspire me to do what I can to help.

Maturation in prayer is marked by *listening*. In Revelation 3:20, Jesus teaches that he is the one who knocks . . . at the door of our hearts, waiting to be welcomed. A good way to pray is to mull over a Scripture passage to hear what God is speaking. The fruit of prayerful listening is knowledge of God's will and the empowerment to say "yes" to it, as Jesus did.

I no longer pray for the Packers. On my better days I pray, "Not my will, but yours be done."

—TS

Meditation: We may think of petitionary prayer as selfish or even unnecessary—doesn't God already know what we need? And yet Jesus constantly encourages us to "ask." Petitionary prayer is neither a philosophical conundrum nor a selfish endeavor—it is a gentle command of Christ, an acknowledgment of our dependence on God, and a testament to the power of prayer. What will you ask for today?

Prayer: Loving God, you know my heart's desires. I lay them before you. Your will be done.

—AE

Stern and Splendid

Readings: Ezek 18:21-28; Matt 5:20-26

Scripture:
Is it my way that is unfair, or rather, are not your ways unfair? (Ezek 18:25b)

Reflection: Today's readings offer us stark lessons early in our Lenten journey: *Sin exists. Judgment exists. We must dig deeper. We must do better.* We hear these lessons, and we cry out with the refrain of today's psalm: "If you, O Lord, mark iniquities, who can stand?" (Ps 130:3).

Indeed Jesus' preaching in today's Gospel seems almost impossible to live up to. Are we liable to judgment and "fiery Gehenna" just for calling someone stupid or foolish? *O Lord, who can stand?* It almost seems un-Jesus-like—so harsh, so demanding, so judgmental!

We may sometimes listen to Jesus and wonder why he's being so hard on us. But we also know, in our heart of hearts, that his words thrill us. We *want* to stop calling people "stupid" and "fools." We want to dig deeper. We want to do better.

As C.S. Lewis so memorably put it, we may think we want an indulgent "grandfather" in heaven, but what we have instead is Love. And Love is "something more stern and splendid." Like the prophets that came before him, Jesus preached truth—a truth that might repel us on its stern surface but that resonates deep within us as good news.

God is offering us a way of life. It is a narrow way, but along this way, as we bite our tongues and work hard and put one journeying foot in front of the other, we are assured that we are never alone: "For with the LORD is kindness / and with him is plenteous redemption" (Ps 130:7).

—AE

Meditation: Digging deeper is what Jesus calls us to throughout the Sermon on the Mount. He invites and challenges us to look within, to root out those things like vicious anger and lust that lead outwardly to sinful words and actions. This rooting out is what allows the Spirit of God who is within us to flourish and to empower us to become the people God calls us to be.

Prayer: Lord, purify my heart and mind of those things that cause me to hurt others. Help me to grow in magnanimity and forbearance, and give me the courage and strength to take the initiative in reconciliation with others.

—TS

Family Likeness

Readings: Deut 26:16-19; Matt 5:43-48

Scripture:
"So be perfect, just as your heavenly Father is perfect."
  (Matt 5:48)

Reflection: Love, in the sense of *agapē*, involves recognizing the dignity of another person as created in God's image; being committed to acting always in the other's best interest; and even being willing to lay down one's life for the other. Such love is a tall order.

We know it can be difficult to love those closest to us—neighbors, people at work, even fellow community or family members. Yet in today's Gospel reading, Jesus commands us to love . . . our *enemies*.

The key to understanding Jesus' teaching here is to look at the reason he offers: "that you may be children of your heavenly Father." He then explains that God sends sunshine and rain on both the good and the bad. The circumference of divine love and blessing knows no bounds.

The logic of Jesus' exhortation to love our enemies is that *agapē*-love is the distinguishing trait of God's family. Some families have a particular physical trait, others a dispositional characteristic, others a vocational tendency. The family of God, manifested by Jesus himself, is marked by self-giving love, a love whose net spreads far and wide, inclusive even of our enemies.

Jesus' final appeal—"be perfect, just as your heavenly Father is perfect"—is best understood in two ways. First, the verb interpreted as "be perfect" contains within it the notion of *process* leading to a goal. I would render it "become perfected," meaning "grow into being a more loving person." Second, the use of the passive voice in "become perfected" is a biblical way of suggesting that the one who makes such love possible is God, through the gift of the Spirit.

—*TS*

Meditation: Identifying ourselves as members of God's family, sharing in the "traits of the family," feels bold. And it should! We have been invited—accepted, adopted, and warmly enfolded—into the divine embrace. And now we are to act like members of this family—loving others with God's love—accepting and enfolding *them*, whether friend or foe. How will you live out this family trait today?

Prayer: Loving God, you have embraced me as a member of your family. Perfect in me the family trait of self-giving love.

—*AE*

Preparing Our Bodies

Readings: Gen 15:5-12, 17-18; Phil 3:17–4:1 or 3:20–4:1;
Luke 9:28b-36

Scripture:
He will change our lowly body to conform with his glorified
body. (Phil 3:21b)

Reflection: A friend e-mailed me an ad for scapulars that
claimed to be "the most comfortable scapulars ever made!"

"Since when were scapulars supposed to be comfortable?"
he quipped, recalling the days when wearing a scapular was
akin to donning a mini-hairshirt: itchy, uncomfortable, and
purposefully so.

For better or for worse, the itchy days have passed. Today
we expect comfort. Even fasting seems to have gone out of
style. This is not necessarily a bad development; Catholics
are not in the business of self-punishment or turning away
from the good things in life. And surely we can all agree that
a true fast consists in serving the poor and refraining from
gossip, much more so than giving up sweets or lattes.

And yet our tradition bursts with examples of physical
fasting. Saints and sinners alike have denied themselves
good things for a time. Many a Bible hero has fasted during
times of intense prayer. But why?

Fasting for a time is a way of preparing our bodies for something our eyes have not seen and our ears have not heard—something beyond even the good things of this world. We're not there yet; we're just on the cusp of it. The transfigured Christ in today's Gospel—face changed in prayer, clothes dazzling white, glorious in appearance—offers us a glimpse of what is to come.

St. Paul tells us that Jesus Christ will change our lowly bodies to conform with his glorified one. That's a moment well worth preparing for.

—AE

Meditation: At Jesus' transfiguration, the Father declares: "This is my chosen Son; listen to him." To listen to Jesus in prayer entails finding time and space for silence. Fasting from those activities and noises that so easily distract us can help us find that time and space. What a difference it makes when we are filled with the life-giving, transforming words of Jesus!

Prayer: Lord Jesus, help me to listen to your words, and by them give me a share in your life.

—TS

How to Be Godlike

Readings: Dan 9:4b-10; Luke 6:36-38

Scripture:
"Be merciful, just as your Father is merciful." (Luke 6:36)

Reflection: In today's Gospel reading, Jesus teaches how we're to be Godlike—as well as how we're *not* to play God. In terms of the latter, Jesus warns against judging and condemning others. If you're like me, this hits close to home.

At one level, Jesus' teaching against judging others is based on the fact that only God knows what lies in people's hearts. Judgment and condemnation are divine prerogatives, not ours. At another level, as the first reading from the prophet Daniel suggests, each one of us stands in need of God's mercy and forgiveness. Psychologists tell us that what we condemn in others is often what we dislike in ourselves. Criticizing others can be a way of deflecting my own sinfulness and failures.

Jesus teaches a different way of regarding others. He instructs his disciples to be merciful, "just as your Father is merciful." In fact, here is another way that we, as God's children, can grow in taking on the divine "family likeness."

A good way to become more merciful is to acknowledge how God has been merciful to me. Daniel's prayer is a confession of sin. Daniel's words can become mine. Observe that those words are directed, in trust, to God who is compassionate and who desires to forgive the contrite. When I truly recognize how merciful God has been to me, it becomes easier for me to look at others with compassion and, even more, to forgive.

The same is true with generosity. When I take time to name the many ways God has blessed me, I become more grateful and am inspired to generosity. In short, I'm inspired to be Godlike.

—TS

Meditation: In theory, it should be easy to receive God's mercy, forgiveness, and generosity. After all, these are things we desperately want. But if we examine our hearts, we may realize that we are resisting these gifts. We may think ourselves undeserving, or we may fear how God's mercy will transform us. Lent is a fruitful time to ask God to soften our hearts, to create fertile ground for God's mercy and generosity, so we may share the fruits of these gifts with others.

Prayer: Merciful God, when I resist your gifts, soften my heart to receive them so I can share them with others.

—AE

Washing Ourselves

Readings: Isa 1:10, 16-20; Matt 23:1-12

Scripture:
Wash yourselves clean!
Put away your misdeeds from before my eyes;
    cease doing evil; learn to do good.
Make justice your aim: redress the wronged,
    hear the orphan's plea, defend the widow. (Isa 1:16-17)

Reflection: We might sometimes wonder where we end and God begins. How does God act in and through us? When we speak or act, when is it our own doing and when is it God's? Of course, there are no clear answers to these questions. Thankfully, the line between God and us is not so clear.

Today's reading from the prophet Isaiah is a wonderful example of this tension between what God does and what we do. Leave it to the prophets to be clear that we are both utterly dependent on God and simultaneously expected to do good and be just and clean. "Wash yourselves!" Isaiah commands.

Wash ourselves? Unexpected words for those of us who hold *God* responsible for doing the washing.

Isaiah's challenging command is golden advice for a good Lent and a good life. *Wash yourself!* This means that we should do the things that cleanse us, that eradicate sin from our lives, that clear our minds of selfishness, evil, and self-centered living. It really only requires one thing, after all: love. Yes, love is the best cleanser there is, better than any soap or disinfectant that money can buy. Love cleans what's on the inside of us, the place that's the dirtiest of all.

Of course, when we do the things that Isaiah exhorts us to do—when we love—we don't know where we end and God begins. When we do good, it is God—it is Christ—doing good through us. When we are cleansed by love, it is God—Christ—who is cleansing us. We do it together. This is love. This is salvation.

—AE

Meditation: Washing ourselves is a way we express our sense of dignity and worth. We get cleaned up before going to work, or to go out with friends, or for special events. We do so to show forth our best selves. From what do I need to be washed to present my best self to God and to others?

Prayer: Lord, wash me with the waters of your love. Cleanse me of all selfishness, resentment, and pride. Help me to recall the cleansing waters of my baptism and to live as a member of the family you form around Jesus.

—TS

Reversing the Calculus

Readings: Jer 18:18-20; Matt 20:17-28

Scripture:
". . . whoever wishes to be great among you shall be your servant." (Matt 20:26)

Reflection: A typical sight at athletic contests is the waving of large foam index fingers signaling the home team's status as "Number One" (at least in their fans' aspirations). It's not just in the world of sports, however, that people vie for first place. Many long for recognition and status, for positions of power and influence.

In today's Gospel, Jesus makes his third and most detailed passion prediction, and the brother apostles James and John seek positions of prestige (in Matthew's version, their mother is the one who makes the request). That something is amiss is evident from clues in the text. The other apostles become upset. But is that because James and John beat them to the request? There are only two places next to Jesus!

The main clue is in Jesus' response to the brothers. He warns against the human tendency, when people have power and authority, to "lord it over" others. Jesus teaches—and lives—another way.

It's important to appreciate that Jesus is all for his disciples striving to be great. However, as is his wont, he reverses the calculus, overturning definitions. Is this any surprise from the one who teaches, "[W]hoever loses his life for my sake will find it" (Matt 16:25)? By losing, we find. By dying, we live.

Here, Jesus redefines what greatness is and what being first entails. It's not a zero-sum, winner-take-all game. Greatness in the kingdom of God is manifested through loving service of others, through giving oneself in love for others. Jesus not only teaches; he puts his teaching into practice, as the one who came "to serve and to give his life . . . for many."

—*TS*

Meditation: Mother Teresa said, "We are called upon not to be successful, but to be faithful." In God's eyes, faithfulness is greatness. And faithfulness to Christ requires humility, compassion, and loving service toward the other. As we continue on our Lenten journey, let us walk this path of greatness. This is how we will come to sit at the right and left of Jesus, where there is room for all.

Prayer: Jesus, give me an open heart so I may learn anew what it means to be great.

—*AE*

Trust in the Lord

Readings: Jer 17:5-10; Luke 16:19-31

Scripture:
Blessed is the man who trusts in the LORD,
   whose hope is in the LORD.
He is like a tree planted beside the waters
   that stretches out its roots to the stream. (Jer 17:7-8a)

Reflection: One evening when only my son Eli and I were at home, I went outside to put something in the car. When I came back in the house, I found Eli at the door, completely distraught. "I thought you were leaving," he said. "I thought I would be alone."

As I hugged Eli and assured him that I wasn't going anywhere, I asked him, "When have I ever left you alone? Why would you think I would do that?"

In today's reading from Jeremiah, God urges us to trust. Like children who don't always know or understand what their parents are up to, God asks for our trust: *"When have I ever left you alone? Why would you think I would do that?"*

Trust is a dynamic reality in relationships, one that ebbs and flows throughout our lives. While some folks cling to God with unwavering trust like the fruitful tree in Jeremiah, most of us experience the uneven growth of a tree in drought and bloom. At times our roots reach out and drink up the cool waters of God's presence. At other times our roots dry up, unable to connect with the very source of our lives.

Our trust in God is not an expectation that God will protect us from every difficulty. Rather, we trust that God will never leave us nor forsake us. Indeed, it is in the times when we feel alone and worried that God is closest to us, embracing and reminding us: *"I've never left you before. I would never do that."*

—*AE*

Meditation: Trust is at the heart of the life of faith. While faith begins with belief, it is nurtured by growing in trust in God to bless and sustain us all our days. The daily practice of taking time to be grateful for the blessings in our lives— both great and small—can help us grow in trusting God. It can also inspire us to recognize and respond to the needs of the Lazaruses around us.

Prayer: Lord, I do trust in you; help my lack of trust. Please make me aware of the ways you constantly embrace me and draw me into your heart. And help me to be a more trust-worthy person for others.

—*TS*

Straightening Crooked Lines

Readings: Gen 37:3-4, 12-13a, 17b-28a; Matt 21:33-43, 45-46

Scripture:
"Finally, he sent his son to them . . ." (Matt 21:37)

Reflection: Today's readings are tales of how human jealousy and resentment lead to violence—and about how God can write straight with the crooked lines of human sinfulness.

Joseph was the favored son of Jacob. To be sure, Jacob was over-the-top in showing his favoritism, and Joseph could be overbearing. But none of that excuses the brothers' hatred of their youngest sibling. When opportunity presented itself, they sought to kill him.

At least Reuben sought a solution that wouldn't involve murder—throwing the young man into a cistern (with the intention of saving him later). But Judah persuaded the brothers to sell Joseph as a captive to traveling Ishmaelites. A blood brother sold, out of jealousy, for twenty pieces of silver.

The story of Joseph continues through many twists and turns. While the brothers' intent was evil, he ended up in a position—as Pharaoh's right hand man, as it were—to save his family and thousands of others from famine. Moreover, Joseph eventually was able to forgive his brothers, seeing how God providentially arranged events so that he became the instrument through whom God rescued many people.

Today's Gospel story is the parable of the rebellious tenants. The landowner's servants were subjected to violence, some to death, when sent to obtain his produce. The most striking feature of the parable is the landowner's decision to send his son. What was he thinking, sending his son into harm's way?!?

God, in great love, holds nothing back from us, not even God's Son. Jesus' death (and resurrection) is the means through which God brings forgiveness and life. Our crooked lines cannot stop God from the work of redemption.

—TS

Meditation: It is comforting to know that even in our sinfulness, we cannot and will not stop God's redemptive work in us and in our world. Of course we always have free will, but God's grace unfailingly abounds. When has your life resembled a crooked line? When did God's steadfastness and love gently straighten those lines, bringing you back into harmony with God's plan for your life? Spend some time today savoring those times in your past and the gratitude that flows in response.

Prayer: Loving God, thank you for writing straight with the crooked lines of my life.

—AE

What We Know About Joseph

Readings: 2 Sam 7:4-5a, 12-14a, 16; Rom 4:13, 16-18, 22; Matt 1:16, 18-21, 24a or Luke 2:41-51a

Scripture:
Jacob was the father of Joseph, the husband of Mary. Of her was born Jesus who is called the Christ. (Matt 1:16)

Reflection: I'll never forget the first time I watched the holiday classic *It's a Wonderful Life.* A friend had urged me to watch it for years, but I never seemed to get around to it. The movie seemed old and dated. What message could it possibly hold for me?

Of course, the movie has a message for everyone. George Bailey thinks his life is a disaster. He feels held back by all of his obligations, his mistakes, and his frustrations. But then, through the visit of an "aspiring angel," George sees what the world would have been like if he had never been born. He sees all the people he's known and how different and empty their lives would have been without him. George understands that his life has value—its value lies in the relationships he has forged, the good he has done, the people he has loved.

We can only hope to be as happy as George Bailey was in those moments of discovery—to see and understand that our lives matter because they touch other lives, to find joy in the ways our lives have intersected with others, to believe that those lives needed ours.

This is the way I think of St. Joseph, whose feast we celebrate today. We know so little about Joseph. But we do know that he was "the husband of Mary" and the father-guardian of Jesus. *We understand Joseph's life in relation to other lives.* And in that way, Joseph is the model human being, a true saint. Joseph wasn't righteous or good in and of himself. He was those things—and more—with others.

—*AE*

Meditation: We have much to learn from Joseph. He is never depicted as speaking, but there is silent eloquence in the selfless care he provided for Mary and Jesus, in the precision of his work as a carpenter, and in many other ways. He is also the model of someone who paid attention to his dreams and followed them.

Prayer: Lord God, who called St. Joseph to care for Mary and Jesus, help me to be faithful in caring for family members and other people you have put into my life. May I be courageous in following the dreams you inspire in me.

—*TS*

Self-Revelation in Love

Readings: Exod 3:1-8a, 13-15; 1 Cor 10:1-6, 10-12; Luke 13:1-9

Scripture:
"This is what you shall tell the Israelites: I AM sent me to you." (Exod 3:14)

Reflection: People who fall in love reveal themselves to one another. The lover desires the beloved to know all about him or her, as well as to learn everything about the beloved. If you are married, recall how this dynamic played out early in your relationship. Alternatively, recall the start of a special friendship. Self-revelation is a manifestation of love.

What is true of human beings, created in God's image, is true of God. God reveals himself to Moses in the burning bush. This momentous episode catalyzed the series of events that led to the creation of God's people in the covenant agreement at Sinai. Moses is encountered and called by God who reveals the divine name, I AM (which renders YHWH). This mysterious name connotes God as the God of life—both as the source of life and the fulfillment of life.

God also reveals his compassionate character as one who hears and responds to the cries of suffering of the enslaved Hebrews in Egypt. This aspect of God's being is reflected in today's psalm response: "The Lord is kind and merciful." Indeed, later in Exodus, God reveals himself again to Moses, now as "a God gracious and merciful, slow to anger and abounding in love and fidelity" (Exod 34:6).

In today's Gospel, Jesus reveals who God is *not*, thereby dispelling a false image of God as punitive and vindictive. Jesus reveals God as patient and compassionate.

Our proper response? *Repentance*, a term that entails changing one's mind and heart. It's essential that we know who God truly is so that we, created in the divine image, show forth to others God's love and compassion.

—TS

Meditation: The divine name I AM derives from the Hebrew verb "to be." The distinct character of YHWH is that God *is*—past, present, and future—and that God causes all things to be. How is God present in your life as a kind and merciful presence and a powerful, creative force? How has God revealed himself to you as I AM?

Prayer: Lord our God, you have revealed yourself to us as one who always has been and always will be with us. May this be the heart of our Lenten journey: your loving presence with us.

—AE

How to Walk Away

Readings: 2 Kgs 5:1-15ab; Luke 4:24-30

Scripture:
But he passed through the midst of them and went away.
(Luke 4:30)

Reflection: There's a hot flame in the Scriptures that's entirely relevant to our contemporary lives—a fire of human anger, a fire of human violence. As we know, people don't always respond to truth—or even love—with calm or joy. Sometimes they respond with outrage.

In today's Gospel reading Jesus speaks a hard truth in Nazareth. The people are "filled with fury." They rise up, driving Jesus out of town, leading him to the brow of a hill with plans to "hurl him down headlong."

This is an angry mob! They are not interested in self-examination or in understanding Jesus. Rather, their instinct is to stop the words they do not want to hear, even if it means killing the messenger. But the messenger—the prophet who has spoken the hard truth—walks away placidly, a model of strength and serenity.

In our contemporary culture, these angry mobs gather and swirl around issues of politics, religion, and morality. Our nation, our Church, and even our families seem divided on so many fronts. And while hurling one another off the brows of hills is uncommon, we have found other ways of hurting and silencing people.

The image of Jesus passing "through the midst of them" and walking away is an instructive one. Sometimes we find ourselves in the midst of human rancor—chaos, disagreement, tension, anger. And while there are times when we must stand in the swirling fury to protect the vulnerable or the truth, at other times we are simply called to pass through it, to walk away with the strength and serenity of Jesus Christ.

—AE

Meditation: Why is it that prophets are not accepted in their native place? One reason, it seems, is lack of humility. Who is he to tell us what to do? Another reason is overfamiliarity. We think we know the prophet, his family, his background. Who does he think he is? Let's not let our familiarity with Jesus get in the way of his surprising us or his challenging us.

Prayer: Lord, open my heart always to welcome you and your words. And please give me the wisdom to know when it is best to walk through the midst of rancor.

—TS

Simple, But Not Easy

Readings: Dan 3:25, 34-43; Matt 18:21-35

Scripture:
"I say to you, not seven times but seventy-seven times."
(Matt 18:21)

Reflection: I had a Scripture professor who, after explaining the meaning of a passage, would often look at us students, smile, and say, "Friends, it's simple . . . but not easy." Typically the passage was one whose meaning was clear. What was challenging was living what the message taught. Today's Gospel reading is one such passage.

Jesus tells the parable of the unforgiving servant in response to Peter's question, "Lord, if my brother sins against me, how often must I forgive . . . seven times?" Let's give Peter some credit; seven times is a generous offer. But Jesus ups the ante—seventy-seven times—and proceeds with the parable.

It's simple to see the disparity between the master's compassion for a servant who begged for forgiveness for a debt he could never repay, and the latter's callous response to a fellow servant who owed him a pittance. Like the onlookers in the parable, we are shaken and enraged.

Now we get to the hard part. While the initial issue seemed to be quantity (seven times?), Jesus' parable is about the *quality* of forgiveness; it must be "from your heart." Why do we find it so difficult to forgive? While some offenses, injuries, and betrayals are grievous (thereby making the difficulty easy to understand), usually the matter is pettier. At times, I like to hold on to resentment. My pride is wounded. Withholding forgiveness can be a way of exacting revenge.

The real problem might be: have I really let the utter gratuity of God's forgiveness sink into my heart? When I do, forgiving others becomes easier. Let's recall this when we pray, "Forgive us our trespasses, *as* we forgive those . . ."

—TS

Meditation: Boxer George Foreman told a story about his painful relationship with his father. One day he realized he had a clear (but not easy) choice: to forgive his father or to simply not have one. Foreman chose forgiveness. When we withhold forgiveness, we miss out on so much. We surrender our peace of mind, forfeit relationships, and turn our backs on God. Forgiving another person is a worthy Lenten offering. Walk on then, and meet Jesus at the cross with an open, forgiving heart.

Prayer: Lord Jesus Christ, forgive me, and grant me a forgiving heart.

—AE

We Remember

Readings: Deut 4:1, 5-9; Matt 5:17-19

Scripture:
"However, take care and be earnestly on your guard not to forget the things which your own eyes have seen, nor let them slip from your memory as long as you live, but teach them to your children and to your children's children." (Deut 4:9)

Reflection: Age and illness can take away our memories. And yet there are some things we never forget, deep down inside. Even as the body may degenerate, even as life skills, relationships, and even personalities may be lost, the core of the person—in the soul—remains unchanged, solid, eternal.

Indeed, those who love and care for the forgetful have seen evidence of this. In my grandmother's final days, her muscle memory responded to the prayers of the priest as—eyes closed and unresponsive—her hand lifted from the hospital bed to make the sign of the cross. This response emerged from deep within, a sacramental sign no doubt learned on the south side of Chicago, in the Irish parish of her childhood.

A friend of mine, a priest with Lewy body dementia, looked at a tree and called it a cross. The ancient symbols of our faith were still known to him, even though he couldn't remember what a fork was for.

We are a people of ritual and sacrament. We repeat prayers and actions, reminding ourselves of things over and over. Our Lenten practice is an example. Every year we pray, we fast, we give of ourselves, we enter into a rich season of liturgy. There are sounds, smells, words, and actions that go with all of it.

No matter what the years may bring, we will never forget these days of ash and worship. Deep inside of us, at the core of our being, we will always remember—we will always be—what we have seen with our eyes, what we have done with our bodies, what we have believed in our hearts, who we are deep within.

—AE

Meditation: "At the core of our being" also gives us insight into today's Gospel reading, where Jesus declares that he has come to fulfill what is taught in Scripture. He fulfills the Scriptures because he incarnates the ways of love taught in the Scriptures, the ways that show forth God's holiness. Jesus does so as God's Son. We, his adopted brothers and sisters, are empowered by the indwelling Spirit to be conformed to Jesus' likeness.

Prayer: Lord, fill me with your Spirit. Give me the "muscle memory" to walk in the way of Jesus.

—TS

Heart of the Matter

Readings: Jer 7:23-28; Luke 11:14-23

Scripture:
If today you hear his voice, harden not your hearts. (Ps 95:8; today's psalm response)

Reflection: Counting up years of studies and my current ministry, I have lived in the Boston area for over twenty years. I never fail to delight in the local accent when Psalm 95 is read at Mass: "If today you hear his voice, *hahhhden nawt your hahhhts*." I hope my amusement, however, never lulls me into failure to heed this warning.

In today's first reading, the prophet Jeremiah is the mouthpiece of God's criticism that the people have not heeded his word; rather, they have walked "in the hardness of their evil hearts" and have not obeyed.

In our Gospel reading from Luke, Jesus is opposed by some in the crowd who accuse him of being able to cast out demons because he is in league with the demonic. Failure to recognize God's love and power at work through the ministry of Jesus is a tragic consequence of hardened hearts.

I like to point out to my students that in Greek, the language of the New Testament, there is a relationship between the words "hear" (*akouō*) and "obey" (*hypakouō*). To obey is, literally, to "hear under." Vis-à-vis God's word, the meaning is to have the humility to *listen*, to recognize that God's words and commands are life. Moreover, when we allow God's words (e.g., through the Scriptures) to take root in and grow in our hearts, we are transformed by their life-giving power. The fruit of such transformation is obedience to God.

Lent is an opportune time to attend to the quality of "soil" in our hearts, just as gardeners these days are turning over the soil of their plots in anticipation of bringing forth flowers and vegetation.

Chowdah, anyone?

—*TS*

Meditation: It can be challenging to discern when we are really hearing God's voice. If we knew for sure that it was God, surely we would obey! God's voice is usually accompanied by peace and a sense of clarity. This does not mean that what God asks of us is easy or instantly makes us happy. Rather, when we hear God's voice, we are at peace, even if what God asks of us is as difficult as death on a cross. Sit in silence today and listen. What do you hear?

Prayer: Speak, Lord, your servant is listening.

—*AE*

Extraordinary, Ordinary Day

Readings: Isa 7:10-14; 8:10; Heb 10:4-10; Luke 1:26-38

Scripture:
Here am I, Lord; I come to do your will. (Ps 40:8a, 9a; today's psalm response)

Reflection: Today's solemnity comes to us in the midst of our Lenten journey, a gentle reminder that at any moment, an ordinary day can become extraordinary.

I wonder what Mary's day was like—the day the light broke in and interrupted her chores, her meal, or her rest. I wonder what she was thinking about, what plans she was making, what she wanted most in her life. I wonder what ordinary things she did that day.

What is your day like today? What are you thinking about? What are you planning, and what do you want? What ordinary things have you done?

Mary's life was not only changed by the light and the angel, or even the great announcement that she would bear a son. Her life (and with it, all of ours) was changed by her deliberate response, one born of prayer and personality, one born of trust: "May it be done to me." Or in the words of the psalmist, "Here I am Lord; I come to do your will."

Let these words be our guide today, and throughout our Lenten journey. *Here I am, Lord!* Let's shout it from our hearts with every fast and with every prayer: *I come to do your will!* If these words are true each day—if we strive to make them true—then we too will change our world with our own response to every shred of light, every wondrous interruption, and every unexpected annunciation in our very ordinary days.

—*AE*

Meditation: God's decision to take on flesh in the person of Jesus depended on Mary's "yes." Her laying aside her own plans to enact God's will is the beginning of the mystery of the Incarnation. Her son Jesus' life was also marked by his "yes" to the Father, as his prayer in the garden, on the night before he gave his life for us, exhibits. May our "yeses" to God, each and every day, bring Christ and his love to others.

Prayer: Lord Jesus, through the intercession of Mother Mary, grant to me the grace and generosity to say "yes" to God and God's ways—each and every day.

—*TS*

Glorification and Sanctification

Readings: Hos 6:1-6; Luke 18:9-14

Scripture:
For it is love that I desire, not sacrifice . . . (Hos 6:6)

Reflection: Vatican II's Constitution on the Sacred Liturgy, *Sacrosanctum Concilium*, teaches that at the Church's liturgy—especially the eucharistic liturgy—two important ends are achieved: the glorification of God and the sanctification of human participants (*SC* 10). This teaching can serve as background for reflecting on Jesus' parable in today's Gospel.

First, I confess that this parable often convicts me, for I find myself thinking, "Thank God I'm not like the Pharisee!" It's tempting to look down on the Pharisee in the same way that the latter dismissed the tax collector. But then we miss the warning about self-righteousness!

We can easily spot what is problematic about the Pharisee's prayer, especially his condemnation of a fellow worshipper and his listing of his own spiritual accomplishments. His prayer is all about himself. But do I at times get so caught up in what I do for God that I (perhaps unwittingly) think that God owes me something?

Here's where glorification and sanctification come in. While implicit, the tax collector glorifies God by humbly recognizing he is in the presence of the divine and by acknowledging his sinfulness. Giving glory, praise, and thanks to God is essential to proper prayer, the appropriate response to all the ways God blesses us. So too is asking for God's mercy.

What about sanctification? How do we know whether our prayer is making us holy? Let me suggest that Paul's list of the "fruit" of the Spirit in Galatians 5:22-23 offers helpful benchmarks: love, joy, peace, patience, kindness, generosity, faithfulness, gentleness, and self-control. Prayer and the sacraments empower us to receive and appropriate these attributes, the marks of Christian holiness—what God desires of us.

—TS

Meditation: Prayer is a relationship—our relationship with God. Prayer can open our eyes to the truth about God and ourselves. When our prayer is humble, authentic, and stripped of pretense, God is glorified, and we are sanctified. This is what God desires—not show, not surface-level devotion, not lip-service. Spend several minutes in silent prayer today. Hold your hands in a position of openness as you pray, signifying your open, sincere heart.

Prayer: "My sacrifice, O God, is a contrite spirit; / a heart contrite and humbled, O God, you will not spurn" (Ps 51:19).
—AE

March 27: Fourth Sunday of Lent

A Ministry of Reconciliation

Readings: Josh 5:9a, 10-12; 2 Cor 5:17-21; Luke 15:1-3, 11-32

Scripture:
. . . God was reconciling the world to himself in Christ, not counting their trespasses against them and entrusting to us the message of reconciliation. (2 Cor 5:19)

Reflection: Anyone who reads the Bible and observes life may wonder why God would trust human beings with anything. We aren't exactly the most trustworthy bunch. But in today's reading from Paul's letter to the (somewhat wayward) Corinthians, Paul insists that God has entrusted us with something terribly precious: the divine work itself, reconciliation.

Paul refers to a "message" and a "ministry" of reconciliation. This is *our* ministry, entrusted to us by the God who has knocked down every obstacle between God and human beings, even death. This is our ministry, entrusted to us by the God for whom reconciliation is the crowning jewel, the precious piece, the thing desired most of all.

Of course, the jury is still out on whether we human beings will faithfully carry out this ministry of reconciliation. It is said that when asked how he thought the "Christian experiment" was going, C.S. Lewis replied, "I don't know. We haven't tried it yet." His wry response reflects what we all know to be true: we have failed to bring the reconciling love of Jesus Christ to bear in our homes, our communities, and our world.

And yet there are glimmers of hope. Every time we think of the other before ourselves, every time we bite our tongue instead of unleashing sarcasm or gossip, every time we sincerely pray for a difficult person, every time we forgive, every time we comfort—in those moments we stand in a dark corner of our world and usher in the warm light of reconciliation. In those moments we practice a sacred ministry—divine in origin, human in application, and infinite in value.

—AE

Meditation: Today's Gospel reading ends with the older brother remaining outside the family residence, mulling over his father's pleading with him to join the feast that celebrates the return of the younger, prodigal son. What will the older brother do? Swallow his pride and go in? Or wallow in his resentment and refuse his father's wish for reconciliation? What would I do?

Prayer: Lord God, who has reconciled the world through Christ and given to your people the ministry of reconciliation, help me to become a reconciled reconciler.

—TS

On Jesus' Terms

Readings: Isa 65:17-21; John 4:43-54

Scripture:
The man believed what Jesus said to him and left. (John 4:50)

Reflection: Starting the fourth week of Lent, the Lectionary sends us to the Gospel of John for the remainder of the season. This Gospel has several particular features, one of which is the careful enumeration of "signs" that Jesus performs that signal his identity as God's Son who came to bring life to the world. Today's reading alludes to the first sign, Jesus' changing water into wine at a wedding in Cana.

Jesus is now back at Cana, where he will perform his second sign. A royal official hears about Jesus and travels a good distance to seek healing for his young son who is at the point of death. We can only imagine the father's anguish at his son's plight. What must his anguish have been upon hearing Jesus' initial response: "Unless you people see signs and wonders, you will not believe"?

Wait a minute! Aren't signs a good thing? Not when people demand them from Jesus. It is not our prerogative to set the terms for divine action in our lives. The mother of God realized this at the wedding when, after Jesus' seemingly off-putting retort—"Woman, how does your concern affect me?"—she exhorted the servers, "Do whatever *he* tells you" (John 2:4-5).

The royal official learns a similar lesson. He has to let go of his expectation that Jesus will accompany him home to heal. Jesus simply says, "You may go; your son will live." Trusting in Jesus' healing power, the man returns by himself, and discovers on the way that his son has been healed. He thereby models a difficult but important lesson: sometimes we must let go and, with trust, let God be God.

—TS

Meditation: On one hand, trust is grace, a gift from God. On the other, it is hard work. Trust is not fostered by asking for signs but by building relationships. This Lent, let's rededicate ourselves to building trust—between ourselves and our Creator, between ourselves and the people in our lives. Let's "let God be God" and receive all the gift and grace that God wishes to give as we do this essential spiritual work.

Prayer: God, I do not ask for anything today. I don't need any signs or wonders. I trust in you, and that is enough.

—AE

Endless Waters

Readings: Ezek 47:1-9, 12; John 5:1-16

Scripture:
The angel brought me, Ezekiel, back to the entrance of the temple of the LORD, and I saw water flowing out from beneath the threshold of the temple toward the east, for the façade of the temple was toward the east; the water flowed down from the right side of the temple, south of the altar. (Ezek 47:1)

Reflection: I grew up in Texas, so I'm no stranger to summer's heat. Of course, as a child, I didn't know anything different. Summers were just hot. But nothing stopped us from being outside.

As a teenager, I learned how dangerous heat can be. A hiking trip in a west Texas desert turned into a life-or-death search for water. Standing on a dusty trail with the sun pelting down on me, the temperature over 100 degrees, and no water in sight, I contemplated death for the first time in my young life. *I might die here,* I remember thinking. *Am I ready?*

I was desperate to find water. But I remember stopping and standing very still, just for a few minutes. I don't remember thinking about how young I was or about all the things I still wanted to do. I just remember thinking about the people in my life, their faces bright and clear in my mind as I thought about them one at a time.

Thinking back on that moment now, I'm touched by it. The desert brought me to a moment of reckoning, when my life boiled down to what mattered most. It was the people.

Today's readings are about water—the healing, life-giving waters of God. The symbolism of water is rich—in the endless waters of God, we are baptized. We die and rise with Christ. We become Church. This is water that fills the soul, a stream that flows on and binds us together.

I still remember how it felt to take that first drink of water on that day in the desert. It felt like life in me.

—AE

Meditation: The man cured in today's Gospel reading "went and told [the religious leaders] that Jesus was the one who made him well." Is he an ungrateful snitch? Not so fast. The verb John uses for "told" is the same verb used elsewhere to announce what Jesus has done to bring us life. How do I proclaim to others the good things God has done to me, including in the waters of baptism?

Prayer: Lord, only you can fill my deep-down thirsts for life and love. Fill me with your Spirit.

—TS

Divine Apprenticeship

Readings: Isa 49:8-15; John 5:17-30

Scripture:
"My Father is at work until now, so I am at work."
(John 5:17)

Reflection: Today's Gospel reading follows upon the third
"sign" Jesus performs, the healing of the paralytic at the pool.
As is often the case in John, Jesus then offers a lengthy discourse that illuminates the significance of the sign.

Because Jesus performs this healing on a Sabbath, a day
of rest sacred to Jews, some religious leaders confront and
challenge him. Jesus responds by saying that, like his Father,
he is now at work to bring forth life. God's creative power
is at work each and every nanosecond (otherwise we
wouldn't exist!), including the Sabbath. In fact, women sometimes give birth on the Sabbath. Life-giving love cannot rest.

Jesus' interlocutors understand exactly what he is suggesting and persecute him for "making himself equal to God."
He then explains, using the imagery of a child-apprentice,
that everything he says and does is what he has heard and
seen from the Father. The image conveys Jesus' intimate
relationship to God and his filial obedience to God's will in
his life and ministry. The Son does not act on his own, but
in full accord with his Father.

Just as the Father has life in himself and gives life, so does Jesus. Moreover, this power to give life extends to resurrection from the dead. God's life-giving, salvific power is grounded in *love*, as the prophet Isaiah proclaims. What Jesus revealed to the paralytic he reveals to us: the tenderness of God's love, the love of the One who never forgets us.

As we move closer to celebrating Easter, let's offer ourselves as apprentice-disciples to Jesus so that we can be "trained" to bear witness to God's love.

—TS

Meditation: Apprenticeship is a helpful analogy for the spiritual life. An apprentice is not expected to be as skilled as the master craftsman—at least not *yet*. But the apprentice is expected to show up every day and be devoted to the craft, no matter how tedious it may be to learn each skill. And so we too arise each day—ready to learn, determined to become more skillful in the holy craft of love.

Prayer: Loving God, teach us your ways so that like Jesus, your Son, we may set about doing your work.

—AE

Golden Calves

Readings: Exod 32:7-14; John 5:31-47

Scripture:
"They have soon turned aside from the way I pointed out to them, making for themselves a molten calf and worshiping it." (Exod 32:8)

Reflection: Today's reading from Exodus tells a vivid story we know all too well. We know it from reading and hearing it—but we've also lived it. This is the story of the people of Israel forming their own god—a "molten calf"—from the melting and reshaping of their own gold in the desert. They made sacrifices to the calf. They reveled before it.

At first the story may seem ridiculous. Didn't the Israelites know that God had rescued them from slavery in Egypt and was leading them to a land flowing with milk and honey? Didn't they appreciate what God had done? Why would they create *another god*?

Of course those questions echo off any hard surface and come right back to us. Why do *we* create other gods? Why are we not satisfied with the One who has liberated us and leads us to better things? Why do we melt our own gold to form something so inferior?

The Israelites did not do this on a whim. They were tired. They felt restless and lost. Weary and distracted, they took their eyes off the prize just long enough to lose their way. We're not so different.

God's wrath burns hot against the sin of the people. But Moses is God's friend (Exod 33:11), and like all good friends, Moses speaks frankly. He urges God to be patient, to "relent" for the sake of the people. And as good friends do, God listens.

God sees every molten calf we make and hears our every reveling cry. But let each one of us take comfort: the "relenting" of God will repeat for as long as we draw breath, for the sake of the people.

—AE

Meditation: What are the "golden calves" today? To what do I give my discretionary time and direct my energies? If the answer is something like a mark of prestige, a professional position, a certain salary figure, etc., I may have a golden calf. Or, when I create a god in *my* image, there is a golden calf. Is there a golden calf in my life?

Prayer: Lord, you are the only and true God. Help me to offer to you—and you alone—praise and glory. Form me in *your* likeness.

—TS

Help on the Journey

Readings: Wis 2:1a, 12-22; John 7:1-2, 10, 25-30

Scripture:
"I know him, because I am from him, and he sent me."
  (John 7:29)

Reflection: Today's readings have ominous overtones that point us toward the culmination of Lent. In the reading from Wisdom, we hear the ruminations of those who plot to destroy an innocent person. In the Gospel text, there are references to those who are trying to kill Jesus and to his "hour" (i.e., the events of Holy Week). However, with an important detail, John also offers light and encouragement.

We learn that Jesus returns to Jerusalem for the Feast of Tabernacles, the setting of the Gospel readings for the next week. The notice of this particular feast takes on significance when we understand what it commemorates and how it was observed. The Feast of Tabernacles (*Sukkot*) is a weeklong autumn celebration that recalls God's guidance and provision for the Israelites during their journey through the wilderness following the exodus.

In Jesus' time, the celebration at the Jerusalem temple involved water libations that symbolized the life-giving waters that would flow from the temple (in accord with visions from the prophet Ezekiel). There were also torch-lit processions at night, presaging the end of nighttime and darkness when God's light would permeate all.

This background can help us appreciate how God has been, and *continues* to be, with us to guide and provide in our journey of Lent and, even more, in the journey of life. God does so through Jesus who, in the following verses, will be presented as providing life-giving waters that truly satisfy (7:37-39, an allusion to the gift of the Spirit) and as "the light of the world" (8:12) who protects us from walking in darkness.

Let's proceed on our journey with great confidence.

—TS

Meditation: Hope is often symbolized by an anchor. Like boats on lakes, we sometimes move in directions we do not expect and are buffeted by winds and storms. A solid anchor provides assurance that we will not be whisked away into oblivion or lost to the power of a storm. Water and light are also symbols of hope. A dark night lit by a torch, a libation of water flowing from the temple: God's light-filled, life-giving presence is with us. We need not fear what lies ahead.

Prayer: Lord my God, make me light, water, and anchor for others, so they too may hope in you.

—AE

The Secret Joy of the Cross

Readings: Jer 11:18-20; John 7:40-53

Scripture:
So a division occurred in the crowd because of him.
(John 7:43)

Reflection: Today's Gospel reading is full of tension and hostility—a cacophony of voices rises up against the person and ministry of Jesus. We see the cross looming on the horizon.

It might surprise and alarm us to note that this roiling tension surfaces here in the seventh chapter of John's Gospel. We are nowhere near the Gospel's end, and yet there is already talk here of "division," of arresting Jesus, of guards and condemnation. Yes, the cross looms early across the life of Jesus.

I grew up in a parish that faithfully celebrated the Stations of the Cross from a rather old-fashioned (and hypnotically beautiful) version of the devotion. Phrases and snippets of it have accompanied me through the years, calling and echoing as I walk along, searching for the way of the cross in my own life. One phrase I have always savored is the suggestion that Jesus took the wood of the cross into his hands "with a secret joy." Why joy? We know why: "it is the instrument with which he is to redeem the world."

In today's Gospel, the crowd, the guards, the chief priests, and the Pharisees all weigh in on who Jesus is, where he came from, and how dangerous he is. The tension is almost too much to bear for us who know what is to come. They will indeed condemn him, lay hands on him, arrest him. And yet, when the wood of the cross touches his hands, a natural dread will be accompanied by a secret joy. The cross that looms across the horizon will become the locus of one man's love—a love with which he will redeem the world.

—AE

Meditation: The Stations of the Cross are a venerable Lenten practice. They capture many poignant moments, such as the suffering Jesus comforting his mother, Veronica's brave and compassionate act of love, Simon of Cyrene helping Jesus bear his cross. Is there a station that grabs your attention or speaks to your heart? That could be where God is leading you to pray during these days.

Prayer: Lord Jesus, following you on the way of the cross is difficult. Give me strength and courage. Open my heart to the immense love your suffering and death reveal.

—TS

A Future of Hope

Readings: Isa 43:16-21; Phil 3:8-14; John 8:1-11

Scripture:
See, I am doing something new! (Isa 43:19)

Reflection: Today's Gospel reading is dramatic. As Jesus teaches in the temple area, suddenly a woman is dragged in and forced to stand in the middle of the crowd. Those who do so claim to have caught her in the act of adultery, though the male partner is conspicuously absent. They intend to show Jesus as "soft" on the Mosaic law that calls for adulterers to be stoned to death.

Take in the scene: the violence (and threat of more violence) the woman experienced, her humiliation, her fear. And what does Jesus do? He bends down and starts writing on the ground with his finger! Guesses abound about what Jesus wrote (as a southpaw, I admit to wondering whether he was left-handed). But what's important is how his action turns down the heat in the face of violent confrontation.

When the leaders persist in pressuring Jesus to take a stand, he challenges them to look into their own hearts, to self-examine their own fidelity to the law. One by one, they walk away, leaving the woman alone before Jesus. And for the first time in the story, her dignity is recognized. Up to this point, she has been used as a pawn. Jesus speaks to her as a person. Even more, he points her to the *future*, a future of hope and new life.

In the second reading, Paul refers to this future as "God's upward calling, in Christ Jesus" (Phil 3:14). Jesus' invitation to the woman enacts what Isaiah, in the first reading, calls God's "doing something new," an allusion to new creation.

What is Jesus calling me to leave behind? How is he inviting me to a future filled with hope?

—TS

Meditation: Memories from the past can cause us pain. The woman in today's Gospel was blessed by the healing presence of Jesus in a traumatic moment. Recall a painful time from your past. Use your imagination and see Jesus there with you. Ask Jesus to heal this time, to transform it forever with his presence. How does this healing prayer infuse your present and even your future with hope?

Prayer: Lord Jesus, I believe that in every moment of my life, you have been with me, healing me, creating me anew, and pointing me toward a future filled with hope.

—AE

Light of the World

Readings: Dan 13:1-9, 15-17, 19-30, 33-62 or 13:41c-62;
John 8:12-20

Scripture:
"I am the light of the world. Whoever follows me will not
walk in darkness, but will have the light of life." (John 8:12)

Reflection: Of all the analogies and symbols in Scripture,
"light" is among those that most resonate with us. Light is
mentioned hundreds of times in the Bible, often in reference
to God. We intuitively understand; the benefits of light are
very much like the grace of God.

Light orients us. As much as my son may want to go out in
the backyard and play football even as night falls, at some
point it simply becomes too dark. He can't see the ball (or
the tree he'll run into!), and I can't see him out the window
to keep him safe. Light helps us see clearly.

Light brings us joy. As the COVID-19 pandemic raged in
the U.S. in 2020, Christmas lights went up earlier than ever
in neighborhoods all over the country. The lights may have
come too early for our liturgical calendars, but they brought
a glimmer of gladness as the days got shorter and we yearned
for signs of good cheer.

Light helps things grow. Like many of you, I'm a gardener.
I live for the first signs of spring—the first buds on the rose

bushes, the tendrils of the clematis vine reaching out for the trellis, the first glorious blue hydrangea of the season. These yearly miracles can't happen without the light and warmth of the sun, closest to us in summer with the leaning of the earth.

Jesus called himself "the light of the world." He's the daylight that gives clarity to our movements, the gentle glimmer of hope in our homes and communities, the light and warmth that bring life to all things.

—AE

Meditation: Another function of light is to expose what is hidden in darkness. The light that Jesus brings can also reveal areas of our lives that need conversion and forgiveness. While we may prefer to keep some things hidden, we know deep down that Jesus' light exposes in order to heal. Where do I need to experience Jesus' healing light?

Prayer: Lord Jesus, you are the Light of the World. Orient me to walk along your paths. Bring joy into my sadness. Shine on me your rays of love to help me grow, and to bring me healing and forgiveness for my sins.

—TS

Lifted Up

Readings: Num 21:4-9; John 8:21-30

Scripture:
"When you lift up the Son of Man . . ." (John 8:28)

Reflection: In today's Gospel reading, we encounter a unique feature of John: the *lifting up* of the Son of Man. In the Synoptic Gospels, Jesus offers three passion predictions (referring to himself as the Son of Man), while in John's version he speaks three times of being "lifted up" (3:14; 8:28; 12:32-34). In fact, in the first instance (3:14), Jesus alludes to the event described in today's first reading: "Just as Moses lifted up the serpent in the desert, so must the Son of Man be lifted up . . ."

The comparison with Moses suggests that, much like those who suffered deadly bites by the seraph serpents as punishment (for complaining against God) received healing by looking at the bronze serpent mounted on a pole, so we receive forgiveness and healing from the "sting" of our sins through Jesus' self-giving death on the cross.

There is another Johannine feature at play. John loves words that have more than one level of meaning. The verb translated "lift up" means, literally, raising something up spatially, as in today's reading—Jesus refers to being raised up on the cross. The same verb, however, also means "exalt."

The cross is the first step in Jesus' being resurrected and exalted in glory.

As we'll see on Good Friday, the cross manifests the full extent of the divine love revealed through Jesus. For that reason, he says, "[Y]ou will realize that I AM" (recall the divine name revealed to Moses) in connection with his being lifted up. In fact, Jesus' first use of "lifting up" is followed by "For God so loved the world that he gave his only Son . . ." (3:16).

John's theology is truly uplifting.

—TS

Meditation: The union of death and exaltation in John's Gospel is a perspective that scatters light across the dark moments of our lives and gives us a sense of what awaits us. Once we take on this perspective, we know that death is never *just death*; it is *death-resurrection-exaltation*. If we are with Jesus on the cross, we will also be with him in resurrection and glory (Rom 6:8).

Prayer: Lord Jesus, lift me up with you, so I may share in your death and your resurrection.

—AE

Shadrach, Meshach, Abednego!

Readings: Dan 3:14-20, 91-92, 95; John 8:31-42

Scripture:
King Nebuchadnezzar said: "Is it true, Shadrach, Meshach, and Abednego, that you will not serve my god, or worship the golden statue that I set up?" (Dan 3:14)

Reflection: The story of Shadrach, Meshach, and Abednego always reminds me of the wonderful song Louis Armstrong sang about them. That gravelly voice and bright trumpet shouted a unique rendition of this ancient story about how "the children of Israel would not bow down." Oh no, Louis sang, you just "couldn't fool 'em with a golden idol"!

Shadrach, Meshach, and Abednego had such faith that they asked nothing of God, even as they were being thrown into the fire. *We would like for our God to save us,* they told King Nebuchadnezzar, *but if God doesn't save us, no matter. We still won't serve* your *god. We still won't worship* your *flimsy golden idol.*

The intrepid faith of Israel is a rich legacy for every Christian. From Moses to Judith to Malachi, the pages of Israel's stories are filled to overflowing with faith—faith that fills time backward and forward, faith that flows like an endless river.

The crowning jewel of Israelite faith is its communal nature. Shadrach, Meshach, and Abednego were not alone, but together. And before Nebuchadnezzar, they represented all of Israel.

Satchmo sang that in the fiery furnace an angel with snow-white wings preached the "power of the gospel" to Shadrach, Meshach, and Abednego. Yes, the gospel is at home in a fiery furnace, sparked by flinty faith. The good news finds fertile ground there, binding us together from age to age.

A lame golden idol is no match for the God of Israel or the gospel of Jesus Christ. Not then, not now!

—AE

Meditation: Our faithfulness in times of trial is more precious than gold refined in fire (1 Pet 1:7). Trials and "fires" come to all of us—whether in the form of sickness, financial hardships, broken relationships, etc. We can be assured that, when the flames of such fires engulf us, we are not alone. The One who shielded the three young men is also beside us, to give us strength and protection.

Prayer: Lord, save me when I am in the fire of trial and testing. Strengthen my faith, and protect me with the fire of your love.

—TS

Learning from Abraham

Readings: Gen 17:3-9; John 8:51-59

Scripture:
"Abraham your father rejoiced to see my day; he saw it and was glad." (John 8:56)

Reflection: The figure of Abraham looms large in today's readings. In the first reading, God bestows the name "Abraham" on Abram, thereby marking a new moment in their relationship. God takes the initiative to establish a covenant with the ninety-nine year old, childless Abraham. In the process, God makes a number of stupendous promises, including countless progeny and "the whole land of Canaan."

In the Gospel reading, Jesus' interlocutors employ the figure of Abraham as a standard of greatness. They do so in response to Jesus' claim that those who keep his word will never die. What Jesus means is that they will never die spiritually. The religious leaders who challenge him understand him as meaning physical death. Abraham, their revered father in faith, died in this sense. Who then is Jesus to make such claims?

Drawing on a tradition that God revealed the future to Abraham (see Gal 3:8), Jesus declares that Abraham foresaw his coming and rejoiced. Moreover, Jesus, who as the Word was with God from the beginning, insists that "before Abraham came to be, I AM" (once again, Jesus self-identifies with the sacred divine name).

Abraham not only functions to make theological points, however. He staked his entire life on God's astounding promises to him. Through Jesus, God has adopted us as his children, has sent the Spirit to indwell us, and has promised us eternal life. We have much to learn from Abraham's response of faith in God.

Another thing we can learn from Abraham is his generous hospitality to the three divine visitors (see Gen 18:1-15). His graciousness can inspire us to welcome God's coming to us in word, sacrament, and one another.

—TS

Meditation: As believers, we "stake our entire lives" on God's astounding promises. With every breath we take, we remind ourselves that our Redeemer lives, and we stand ready to give a reason for our hope (1 Pet 3:15). Which of God's promises do you cling to today? How do you speak this promise into a world that yearns for a reason to hope?

Prayer: God of our ancestors in faith, your ancient promises are new for me each morning. Like Abraham, I cling to your promises; I breathe them; I proclaim them with my life.

—AE

Is God Faithful?

Readings: Jer 20:10-13; John 10:31-42

Scripture:
In my distress I called upon the Lord, and he heard my voice.
(Ps 18:7; today's psalm response)

Reflection: Scripture scholar Walter Brueggemann has said that the entire Bible revolves around a single question: *Is God faithful?* The people, the prophets, the heroes, and the sinners are all asking it. We ask it, too.

This is one reason that Jesus' life is so revealing. In today's Gospel, a crowd of people "pick up rocks" to throw at him. Jesus' life was always heading toward the brow of a hill, a religious tribunal, or a Roman punishment.

Of course, Jesus' life was always heading right where our own lives are heading—to death. And the prospect of death naturally prompts us to ask if God is faithful. *Did God give us everything only to ask for everything back?* So much is unknown; so much is uncertain. The surrender almost crushes us.

Faced with the harsh reality of Lazarus's death, Jesus groaned deep in his soul (John 11:33). At the prospect of his own death, he was troubled, distressed, and agitated (Mark 14:33). Matthew's Gospel says that in the garden Jesus threw himself on his face (26:39). And yet, his entire life declared that *God is faithful*. With every word, every exorcism, and every healing, with every meal eaten in the company of sinners, Jesus was determined to share the intimate connection with the ever-faithful Father that defined his own life.

Our own lives may walk a meandering path, one that weaves in and out of awareness of God's faithfulness. At times we're sure; at times we're not. We'll groan like Jesus, we'll be troubled, we'll lie face down in the dirt of the garden. But in the end, I believe that we too will declare it: *God is faithful*.

—*AE*

Meditation: How do we know that God is, and will continue to be, faithful? A brief meditation on the Trinity can help. God so loved us that he sent his only Son for our salvation. God's love is such that God holds nothing back from us. Jesus held nothing back in revealing God's love, offering his life for us. Moreover, God sends the Spirit, the eternal bond of love between Father and Son, into our hearts. God is committed to us.

Prayer: Faithful and loving God, increase my trust in you. Strengthen my faith, and deepen my commitment to do your will.

—*TS*

Johannine Irony

Readings: Ezek 37:21-28; John 11:45-56

Scripture:
". . . it is better for you that one man should die instead of the people." (John 11:50)

Reflection: The evangelist John's love of irony is evident in two ways in today's Gospel reading. The first is in connection with "signs," as members of the Sanhedrin (the supreme religious and judicial council of Jews) acknowledge: "This man is performing many signs."

The most recent is the raising of Lazarus from the dead, the recounting of which immediately precedes today's reading (11:1-44). Jesus, who is "the resurrection and the life," summons his friend Lazarus—already four days in the tomb—back to life. But it's not enough that Lazarus's heart beats and his lungs breathe; he appears at the tomb's entrance still bound by his burial clothes. Jesus' command to the onlookers—"Untie him and let him go"—illustrates something he said in the Good Shepherd discourse: "I came that they may have life and have it more abundantly" (10:10).

While this sign points to Jesus' divine life-giving power, the religious leaders regard it as a threat to their power and authority. They swiftly decide that he must die. Jesus' raising a man back to life leads to his own death sentence. Ironic indeed.

So too are the words, quoted above, of the high priest Caiaphas. His meaning was pure political expediency (sadly, the tendency to respond with violence to perceived threats to power lives on today). However, the high priest spoke much more than he knew. Jesus' death *is* for the salvation of the world. His being lifted up "will draw everyone to [him]" (12:32).

We now stand on the cusp of Holy Week and the celebration of the Paschal Mystery, of God's bringing life through the death and resurrection of Jesus.

—TS

Meditation: As we prepare to enter into the most sacred days of the liturgical year, we pause to take stock of our Lenten experience thus far. Let us consider, one at a time, the Lenten pillars of prayer, fasting, and almsgiving. In which of these areas have we been most faithful? What efforts, what silence, what service can we intensify as these days unfold?

Prayer: Jesus, keep us close to you in the days ahead. Raise up what is dead in us. Speak to us of resurrection and life.

—AE

Enter the Story

Readings: Luke 19:28-40; Isa 50:4-7; Phil 2:6-11; Luke 22:14–23:56 or 23:1-49

Scripture:
[A]nd now as he was approaching the slope of the Mount of Olives, the whole multitude of his disciples began to praise God aloud with joy for all the mighty deeds they had seen. (Luke 19:37)

Reflection: As a mother of four, I can tell you what happens with palms on Palm Sunday. They hit you in the face during Mass, they fall on the dirty floor of the church and are retrieved, they are sat upon and torn and folded into crosses (or numerous attempts to do so are made and abandoned). They are passed down the row, held in the air, wiggled and waved, gripped in palms of every size, from largest to smallest.

Waving palms on Palm Sunday is an old tradition. We do it like we do so many things in liturgy—with our bodies as well as our minds, hearts, and voices. We feel the smoothness of the palm in our hands, we see its sleek lines and its pale green color, we feel the air move as we wave it, we see how many fill the church, we feel the energy in the room.

With this day—with this movement and this liturgy—we move into the dance, the ceremony of Holy Week. When we reach out and take the palm, we commit ourselves to an ancient story and our part in it. We become the crowd.

The Pharisees were scandalized by the shouting and praising and joy of the welcoming crowds, all because of Jesus. They told Jesus to silence his disciples, to make the people stop, as he approached the Mount of Olives. But Jesus didn't stop the people, and he won't stop us.

We know what is to come. But for today, for now, we take up palms. We pass them down the row. We place one in every hand, largest to smallest. We enter the story.

—AE

Meditation: We hear two Gospel readings today: Jesus' triumphant entry into Jerusalem and the passion story. The people who jubilantly welcome Jesus yell, a few days later, "Crucify him!" Their fickleness contrasts with Jesus' faithfulness. He enters the city riding on a beast of burden, not on a warhorse. In death, he embodies what he has taught: loving and forgiving his enemies; reaching out in mercy to the marginalized (i.e., the repentant criminal); praying with trust to his Father.

Prayer: Lord Jesus, as I hold my palm, help me to recall your faithfulness-and-love-unto-death.

—TS

Anointed

Readings: Isa 42:1-7; John 12:1-11

Scripture:
"Let her keep this for the day of my burial." (John 12:7)

Reflection: We so easily refer to Jesus as "Christ" that the latter is tantamount to a last name. "Christ" is not a surname, however, but a title. It means "Anointed One," typically rendered "Messiah." At the beginning of his ministry, Jesus interprets the outpouring of the Spirit at his baptism as an anointing that will lead him to bring good news to the poor, sight to the blind, and freedom to captives (Luke 4:14-21; cf. Isa 61:1-2).

In today's Gospel, near the end of his life and ministry, Jesus receives another anointing, from Mary of Bethany. Mary's anointing with costly oil is an extravagant gesture of love for Jesus, who defends her gesture, interpreting it as an anticipatory burial anointing. Messiah he is, but one whose mission includes suffering and death.

The first reading, from Isaiah, is the first of four songs of "the Servant of the Lord." We will hear all four Servant Songs during Holy Week, culminating on Good Friday. From early on in the Church (likely starting with Jesus himself), the Servant described in these songs has been understood to illuminate Jesus' ministry and, especially, his suffering and death.

Today's reading evokes much of what Jesus set forth at the outset of his ministry—e.g., opening the eyes of the blind, bringing forth captives from the dungeon. The song also accents the Servant's nonviolence and gentleness ("Not crying out, not shouting, / . . . A bruised reed he shall not break"). The gentleness of the Servant is not weakness, but rather is an expression of power, the power of love.

Something to keep in mind throughout the week as we prayerfully contemplate Jesus, the suffering Messiah.

—TS

Meditation: Mary used so much oil to anoint the feet of Jesus that "the house was filled with the fragrance of the oil." Her extravagance was in proportion to her love. How will we give extravagantly to Jesus? With what act of service will we show our boundless love this Holy Week?

Prayer: Jesus, the presence of your friends Mary, Martha, and Lazarus was a comfort to you as you neared the end of your life. May we be a comforting presence to all we encounter, ready to relieve their suffering in any way we can.

—AE

April 12: Tuesday of Holy Week

An Endless Moment

Readings: Isa 49:1-6; John 13:21-33, 36-38

Scripture:
Reclining at table with his disciples, Jesus was deeply troubled . . . (John 13:21a)

Reflection: Few scenes in Scripture are as intimate as Jesus' last meal with his disciples. We imagine them in a darkened room, candles flickering, a small space, quiet voices. We wonder what everyone was thinking and feeling.

Jesus had been predicting his death, and now he speaks of betrayal and of going away. There was surely an intensity about him that the disciples would have detected. Today's Gospel tells us that, sitting at the table with his disciples, Jesus was "deeply troubled."

To imagine Jesus troubled is both comforting and disturbing. The evangelists do not shield us from the emotions of Jesus. During his ministry, we see anger, exasperation, and grief. As death draws near, we see dread, distress, and a troubled spirit. Neither life nor death is easy.

The moments in the Upper Room were precious ones between Jesus and his friends. True, the moments were filled with misunderstanding, confusion, and even betrayal. And yet the bond of living and traveling together, of listening and learning—of loving one another—filled the room, too. I like to think time was suspended for those seemingly endless moments: eating together one last time, praying and singing ancient songs, the quiet murmuring of conversations, the instant hush when Jesus spoke.

Have we ever had such an endless moment with Jesus of Nazareth? Have we hushed our own souls to listen? Will we enter into his distress and allow our own emotions to create intimacy between ourselves and Jesus as the cross draws near?

—AE

Meditation: Intimacy with Jesus is also signaled in the Gospel reading by the reference to the disciple "whom Jesus loved" resting against his chest. The beloved disciple is never named in John's Gospel. One reason is that he serves as a model for *all* of Jesus' disciples. As John depicts Jesus in the Prologue as being at the Father's bosom from eternity (1:18), so now he employs the same word, *kolpos*, to describe the beloved disciple's resting against Jesus' chest. Each one of us is invited to that intimacy with the One who tenderly washes our feet and offers himself to us as the Bread of Life.

Prayer: Lord Jesus, draw me close to you. Help me to live as your beloved disciple.

—TS

April 13: Wednesday of Holy Week

Betrayal

Readings: Isa 50:4-9a; Matt 26:14-25

Scripture:
"Amen, I say to you, one of you will betray me." (Matt 26:21)

Reflection: When I was young, I remember getting a kick out of hearing Wednesday of Holy Week referred to as "Spy Wednesday." It sounded so cool, full of intrigue. And intrigue there is, as Judas confers with the religious leaders about an asking price. But the reality is that today's Gospel reading is about betrayal, and there is nothing cool about that.

Jesus is betrayed by an intimate, by one whom he chose to be an apostle, by one who had accompanied him throughout his ministry of proclaiming God's kingdom. He is betrayed by one with whom he had shared bread many times; indeed, in today's reading, Judas "dipped his hand into the dish with [Jesus]." And, as the story proceeds, Judas will identify Jesus as the one to be arrested by offering a kiss, a gesture that grossly twisted its typical conveyance of peace.

The purpose here is not to pile on Judas, but to highlight what a terrible thing betrayal is. Sadly, betrayal is something that many people experience. These can take consolation knowing that they have as Lord one who empathizes with them. One who, as the third Servant Song from Isaiah declares, knows how to speak to the weary a word that will encourage them.

The betrayal of Jesus was the beginning of many sufferings he bore on his way to the cross. Like the Servant, he was able to endure because he knew God's help.

As we arrive at the Easter Triduum, we will have occasion to see that, while betrayal sets in motion the saving events we will celebrate, it does not have the final word. God's love and power to save through Jesus have the last say.

—TS

Meditation: Jesus has experienced the pain of strained or broken relationships: the betrayal of Judas, the sleepiness of his friends in the garden, their desertion at his arrest and death. Human relationships are messy; Jesus is no stranger to that fact. Offer Jesus a relationship in your life that is in need of healing. Pray this week that the reconciling love of the cross may have the final word.

Prayer: Jesus, forgive my betrayals, my sleepiness, and my desertion. Replace my weakness with faithfulness so that even when I sleep, my heart will be awake with you (Song 5:2).

—AE

All Things Converge

Readings: Exod 12:1-8, 11-14; 1 Cor 11:23-26; John 13:1-15

Scripture:
In the same way also the cup, after supper, saying, "This cup is a new covenant in my blood. Do this, as often as you drink it, in remembrance of me." (1 Cor 11:25)

Reflection: One could argue that every essential theme of the Bible converges on Holy Thursday—on this holy night that is like no other, a night when a new covenant was cut and an old one deeply cherished. Where do we begin to wrap our minds around what happened on this night?

The yearly celebration of Passover, a "perpetual institution," has for countless generations been the great "memorial feast" of Judaism (Exod 12:14). It is a celebration of liberation and love, a night when Israel lays claim to a special status: the liberated people of God. The consumption of the roasted lamb and the bitter herbs, and the retelling of the great story of the exodus, are a living memory of a moment in time that declares for all eternity that God cares for what God has made.

At his last meal with his disciples, through both meal and service, Jesus perpetuated this living memory and called it "new." A Passover meal was celebrated with new symbolism that did not negate the old, but built upon it. The Master washed the feet of his disciples—another living symbol that spoke profoundly of God's own self-giving, God's willing condescension, God's deep love for what is small and humble.

Covenant, meals, service, humility, love that does not count the cost—all sacred things converge on Holy Thursday. With all of the created world—past, present, and future—let us rejoice on this holy night as God takes care of what God has made.

—AE

Meditation: Among many things, the Mass on Holy Thursday celebrates the gift of the Eucharist—Jesus' broken Body and poured out Blood—to the Church. Interestingly, the Gospel account we read tonight is the only one that focuses on *another* action at the Last Supper, Jesus' washing the feet of his disciples. The liturgy thereby teaches that a eucharistic people should be characterized by their loving service of one another.

Prayer: Lord Jesus, I thank you for the most precious gift of your Body and Blood in the Eucharist. May it inspire and empower me to offer foot-washing love to my brothers and sisters.

—TS

Love Perfected

Readings: Isa 52:13–53:12; Heb 4:14-16; 5:7-9;
John 18:1–19:42

Scripture:
"It is finished." And bowing his head, he handed over the
spirit. (John 19:30)

Reflection: My mentor and friend, the late Daniel J. Har-
rington, SJ, used to remark that the Good Friday liturgy was
his favorite. It is mine, too. What a privilege to see the faces
of people as they venerate the cross. Those faces reflect a
myriad of emotions and feelings—sorrow and suffering on
the one hand; gratitude and tender love on the other.

As Scripture scholars, I think Dan's and my bias towards
Good Friday is that the Liturgy of the Word is so prominent.
And what a wealth of riches to contemplate: the fourth Servant Song from Isaiah; the image of Jesus as high priest who
sympathizes with our weaknesses; and the passion according
to John.

Let's focus on Jesus' last words. First, he looks down from
the cross at his mother and the beloved disciple. Even in his
torment, Jesus offers comfort to and provides for his mother.
His words to both figures symbolize the family of faith he
has created, the family of the Church that will be nourished
by the sacraments, signified by the outpouring of water and

blood from his pierced side. Next, Jesus cries out, "I thirst." Physical thirst, certainly. But even more, his thirst that we receive his offer of love.

It's that offer of love that is reflected in Jesus' last words: "It is finished." The Greek verb here connotes more than an ending; it means bringing something to its accomplishment, even to perfection. Jesus came to reveal the love of God. The cross, upon which Jesus opens wide his arms, expresses most fully the extent of his love for us.

No wonder people are so reverent when venerating the cross.

—TS

Meditation: Spend some quiet time in prayer before a cross today—at church, at home, or even outside. Meditate on Jesus' words: "I thirst." Jesus was experiencing the excruciating discomfort of a man dying a violent death—and the deep spiritual yearning for a connection with each of us. Your presence, your time with Christ crucified, is a response to his thirst.

Prayer: Jesus, as I venerate your cross today, I imagine your arms outstretched, a sign of your great love for me and for all people. You have given yourself completely, perfectly. It is finished.

—AE

Journey to the Tomb

Readings: Easter Vigil: Gen 1:1–2:2 or 1:1, 26-31a;
Gen 22:1-18 or 22:1-2, 9a, 10-13, 15-18; Exod 14:15–15:1;
Isa 54:5-14; Isa 55:1-11; Bar 3:9-15, 32–4:4; Ezek 36:16-17a,
18-28; Rom 6:3-11; Luke 24:1-12

Scripture:
At daybreak on the first day of the week the women who
had come from Galilee with Jesus took the spices they had
prepared and went to the tomb. (Luke 24:1)

Reflection: Our Lenten journey has brought us here, to this
quiet moment of "already but not yet." It is a place where
we are strangely comfortable, and yet perpetually uncomfortable. Comfortable because we are so accustomed to living
"in-between." Uncomfortable because we want to finally
arrive.

Tonight's vigil, with its litany of ancient readings, begins
with the spirit of God sweeping across the waters. With that
first command of God that light be scattered across our
world, a drama of relationship, covenant, and redemption
began. That drama plays out in our everyday lives, in chapels
and churches, even more in kitchens and cubicles.

The last reading of tonight's vigil is the Gospel which begins, fittingly, with a reference to "daybreak." From light to
light we go, searching for the glory of the risen Christ.

The women come to the tomb expecting to find a dead body, ready to anoint it. But the body is not there. Peter, running to the tomb, also seems to expect a body: bending down and looking inside, he sees for himself the emptiness of the tomb, the burial clothes cast aside.

Holy Saturday is a day when we accept and even celebrate the "in-between" reality of our lives. We *know* he is raised. We *have seen* his glory! And yet we still come to the tomb again and again, prepared for something different—just in case—needing to see for ourselves.

This is the empty tomb, where the Spirit of God hovers, where the light has broken in. Our journey has brought us here. We have arrived.

—*AE*

Meditation: The Easter Vigil is the pinnacle of liturgical celebrations. In addition to the litany of Scripture readings, we experience the lighting of the paschal fire, the clanging of bells and joyous singing of *Alleluia*, the proclamation of the Exsultet, and the celebration of Sacraments of Initiation as we welcome new members into our communities. All in celebration of the victory of Christ over the grave. How have I experienced new life at Easter celebrations?

Prayer: God of life, open our hearts to the newness of life we celebrate. Thank you for leading us on our Lenten journey. Help us to bear witness with our joy to the resurrection of your Son.

—*TS*

More than a Day

Readings: Acts 10:34a, 37-43; Col 3:1-4 or 1 Cor 5:6b-8;
John 20:1-9

Scripture:
"This man God raised on the third day . . ." (Acts 10:40)

Reflection: Easter Sunday. I confess, however, to a puzzlement I used to have at the morning Mass on this day. The Gospel reading seems a bit muted. Mary of Magdala discovers that the tomb is empty and races to tell Simon Peter and the beloved disciple, who confirm her discovery.

Notice, however, that there is no appearance by the risen Jesus. Nor any announcement by angels at the tomb that Jesus has been raised from the dead. The final verse even states that the disciples "did not yet understand the Scripture that he had to rise from the dead." This is Easter Sunday, for crying out loud. Why not more fireworks?!?

There *is* the detail about Peter's seeing the burial cloths, with the cloth that covered Jesus' head rolled up in a separate place. A most significant detail! It's John's way of suggesting, even at this early moment in the story, that something marvelous is afoot. Jesus has put aside the cloths of death's sleep, folding them up like pajamas, and has left the tomb for good.

What I've come to appreciate is that the mysteries of Easter—God's vindication of all that Jesus taught and did;

the victory of life over death; the overcoming of sin by grace—are so marvelous that one day cannot do them justice. In fact, Easter "Day" is an octave of eight days in the Church's liturgy. We have this entire week to hear the stories of the appearances of the risen Jesus to his followers. Moreover, we have fifty days to joyfully celebrate Easter, culminating in the feast of Pentecost, God's outpouring of the Spirit of life.

The Lord is risen; he is risen indeed!

—TS

Meditation: The empty tomb is a profound symbol of Christian faith. The emptiness is its own Easter proclamation: there is no death here! We may yearn for that encounter with the Risen One, but it is not required. We do not need proof— we *believe*. The tomb of Christ is not the dark end but the light-filled beginning.

Prayer: Lord Jesus Christ, Risen One, we offer you every thought of our minds, every step of our feet, every loving action of our hands, and every prayer we have spoken on this Lenten journey. As we stand in the emptiness of this wondrous tomb, fill us with your light and love as we proclaim your resurrection from the core of our being: *Alleluia! Alleluia! Alleluia!*

—AE

References

March 7: Monday of the First Week of Lent
St. John of the Cross, *Dichos* 64. Also quoted in *Catechism of the Catholic Church* 1022.

March 11: Friday of the First Week of Lent
C.S. Lewis, *The Problem of Pain* (New York: Harper One, 1996), 31–32.

March 16: Wednesday of the Second Week of Lent
Navin Chawla. "The miracle that was Mother Teresa." *The Hindu* (Aug. 26, 2011).

April 2: Saturday of the Fourth Week of Lent
Rev. Loren Gavitt, ed., *Saint Augustine's Prayer Book: A Book of Devotion for Members of the Episcopal Church,* revised edition (West Park, NY: Holy Cross Publications, 1990).

April 8: Friday of the Fifth Week of Lent
"It's Not a Matter of Obeying the Bible: 8 Questions for Walter Brueggemann," interview with Marlena Graves (January 9, 2015), http://marginalchristianity.blogspot.com/2015/01/its-not-matter-of-obeying-bible-8.html.

SEASONAL REFLECTIONS NOW AVAILABLE IN ENGLISH AND SPANISH

LENT/CUARESMA

Not By Bread Alone: Daily Reflections for Lent 2022
Amy Ekeh and Thomas D. Stegman, SJ

No sólo de pan: Reflexiones diarias para Cuaresma 2022
Amy Ekeh and Thomas D. Stegman, SJ;
translated by Luis Baudry-Simón

EASTER/PASCUA

Rejoice and Be Glad:
Daily Reflections for Easter to Pentecost 2022
Susan H. Swetnam

Alégrense y regocíjense:
Reflexiones diarias de Pascua a Pentecostés 2022
Susan H. Swetnam; translated by Luis Baudry-Simón

ADVENT/ADVIENTO

Waiting in Joyful Hope:
Daily Reflections for Advent and Christmas 2022–2023
Mary DeTurris Poust

Esperando con alegre esperanza:
Reflexiones diarias para Adviento y Navidad 2022–2023
Mary DeTurris Poust; translated by Luis Baudry-Simón

Standard, large-print, and eBook editions available. Call 800-858-5450 or visit www.litpress.org for more information and special bulk pricing discounts.

Ediciones estándar, de letra grande y de libro electrónico disponibles. Llame al 800-858-5450 o visite www.litpress.org para obtener más información y descuentos especiales de precios al por mayor.